HAPPY NEW YEAR,
EVERYWHERE!

HAPPY NEW YEAR, EVERYWHERE!

ARLENE ERLBACH

ILLUSTRATED BY SHARON LANE HOLM

THE MILLBROOK PRESS   BROOKFIELD, CONNECTICUT

For the New Year's People

Steve, Karen & Paul Arnold

Margie Freeman

Leonard, David & Rachel Levin

Chuck, Elyse & Meghan O'Connor

Herb & Matt Erlbach

Hope we have many more celebrations together.

—AE

To Chrissy—forever friends.

—SLH

Published by The Millbrook Press, Inc.
2 Old New Milford Road, Brookfield, CT 06804
www.millbrookpress.com

Library of Congress Cataloging-in-Publication Data
Erlbach, Arlene.
Happy New Year, everywhere! / by Arlene Erlbach;
illustrated by Sharon Lane Holm.
p. cm.
Includes bibliographical references.
Summary: Describes New Year greetings and customs from
twenty countries and includes games, recipes, and crafts projects.
ISBN 0-7613-1707-4 (lib. bdg.)
1. New Year—Juvenile literature. [1. New Year. 2. Holidays.]
I. Holm, Sharon Lane, ill. II. Title.
GT4905 .E75 2000
394.2614—dc21   99-057335

CONTENTS

ACKNOWLEDGEMENTS

This book would not have been possible without help from all these wonderful people.

Afrique Magazine and Andrew Eperi
The Akintunde Family
The Australian Consulate
Bass Communications
The Consulate General of Belgium
Ms. Brigid Boddin
Ms. Susan Bouldrey
Ms. Cécilia Brady
The Consulate General of Brazil
The Embassy of Brazil
The British Consulate
Professor Caballo
The Canadian Consulate
Ms. Janet Carlson
The Embassy of Chile
Chinatown Chamber of Commerce
The Chinese American Service League
Ms. Veronica Cobo
Ms. Rosa Cruz
Ms. Carol Erlbach
Mr. Herbert Erlbach

The Embassy of Ethiopia
The Consulate General of Germany
The Embassy of Ghana
The Consulate General of Haiti
Ms. Jean Halevi
Ms. Lois Harris
Ms. Patricia Harris
The Hellenic Museum and Cultural Center
The Consulate General of India
The Iranian American Society
Ms. Marlene Julien
The Japanese Consulate
The Embassy of Mexico
The Embassy of Nigeria
Dr. Samuel Quartey
Mrs. Sato
Mr. Baba Sisse
The Embassy of Trinidad & Tobago
The Vietnamese Association of Chicago
The Vietnamese Association of Illinois

INTRODUCTION

Sometime during the year, all over the world, children say good-bye to the old year—and then they welcome a new one. They are following the ancient custom of celebrating New Year's, one of the world's oldest holidays.

Thousands of years ago people did not have calendars. They counted time by following nature's changes. Certain events made them think that an old year had passed and a new one had begun. Some people marked the new year by the warming of the Earth each spring. Others felt that it occurred when rains came and watered crops. Some people believed a new year began at the harvest.

People assumed that gods in the sky controlled these occurrences. To thank the gods and ensure another good year, people honored the gods with festivals. They left gifts of crops, flowers, or animals for the gods. They hosted feasts, sang songs, and held parades to show the gods how much they appreciated them. When you watch the New Year's Day parade on TV, or celebrate with noisemakers and hats, you are following a modern version of one of the world's oldest customs.

Not everyone observes New Year's exactly as you do. In some other cultures, the new year arrives in the spring, summer, or fall. People may welcome it with different customs.

In this book you'll discover many games, food, and crafts that make New Year's special all over the world. You can add some of these activities to your own celebration—or you can welcome New Year's a few times a year. Whenever you celebrate the new year, you share a tradition with people all over the world. You are honoring a time that has passed and a new one that is about to begin.

Arlene Erlbach

BELGIUM

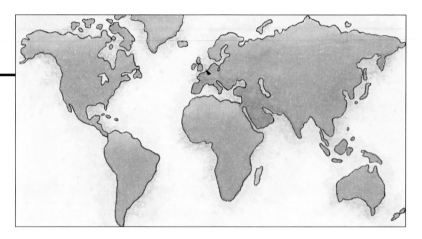

DATE: December 31 & January 1

NAME: New Year or Saint Sylvester Day

GREETING: *Gelukkig Niewjaar* (Happy New Year) Pronounced heh-look-EH-hah new-YAR. The greeting is in Flemish, the language of northern Belgium. The French-speaking people of Belgium say *Bonne Année*, pronounced bun ah-NAY.

If you lived in southern Belgium, you'd complete a special project on December 31: a New Year's letter to your parents. Belgian children work on their letters from the day after Christmas to December 31. The letters express thanks to their parents and contain promises about their plans for the new year. The children decorate their letters with drawings, stickers, and glitter. On New Year's Day, each child in the family stands on a chair and reads the letter to his or her parents to show them how much they're appreciated.

You can make a New Year's letter for your parents. Here's how to do it.

Directions for making **NEW YEAR'S LETTERS:**

WHAT YOU'LL NEED:

colored construction paper

sheets of lined paper

a pen or a fine-tipped marker

glue

stickers

glitter pens

crayons or markers

scissors

WHAT TO DO:

1 Cut the lined paper in half. This way there will be plenty of room for a border when you attach the letter to the construction paper.

2 Practice writing your letter to your parents until it's in your best handwriting. Thank them for what they've done for you this year. Remember to add your promises for the new year.

3 When your letter is written in your best handwriting, glue it to the construction paper.

4 Decorate the border with stickers, glitter, or drawings.

5 On New Year's Day, stand on a chair. Read the letter to your parents.

Dear Mom & Dad

Thank you for taking care of me.
I promise to study and get good grades and make you proud of me in the New Year.

love,
Alexandra
xo

9

BRAZIL

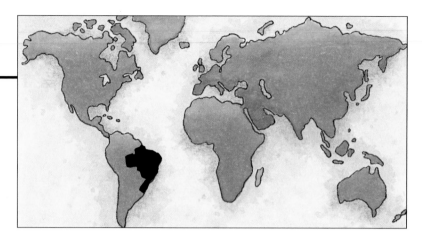

DATE: December 31 & January 1

NAME: Ano Novo

GREETING: *Feliz Ano Novo* (Happy New Year)
Pronounced fay-LEES AH-noh NOH-voh. Although Brazil is located in South America, where most people speak Spanish, Brazil's language is Portuguese.

At midnight on New Year's Eve, people in southern Brazil go to the beach. They light candles and place them in the sand to honor Iemanjá, the sea goddess. Some people scatter flower petals on the beach for her. Others give Iemanjá jewelry, perfume, or fruit. They throw their gifts into the water or put them on tiny boats. If the items float out to sea, people believe that Iemanjá will grant their wishes.

On New Year's Eve or New Year's Day, Brazilian people often eat a meal featuring turkey, chicken, or ham served with lentils—and *rabanada* for dessert. Rabanada is similar to French toast. You can make rabanada on New Year's Eve or New Year's Day for a special treat.

Directions for making **RABANADA:**

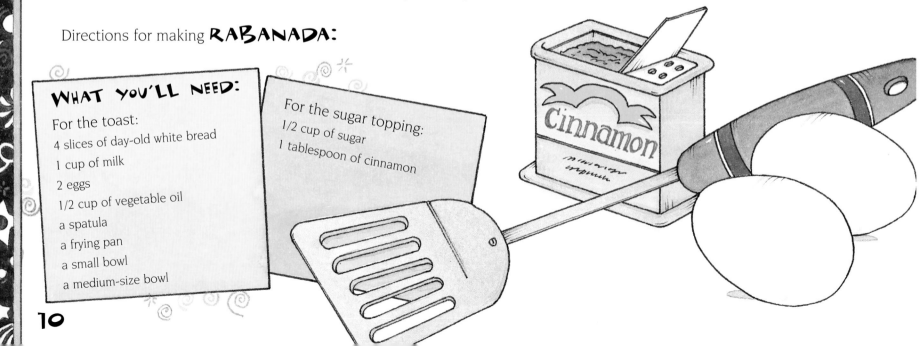

WHAT YOU'LL NEED:

For the toast:
4 slices of day-old white bread
1 cup of milk
2 eggs
1/2 cup of vegetable oil
a spatula
a frying pan
a small bowl
a medium-size bowl

For the sugar topping:
1/2 cup of sugar
1 tablespoon of cinnamon

WHAT TO DO:

 1 Mix the cinnamon and sugar into the small bowl. Set aside.

 2 Beat the eggs and milk together in the medium bowl with an electric mixer or egg beater.

 3 Cut each slice of bread into four triangles.

 4 Have an adult heat the oil in the frying pan.

 5 Dip the bread triangles into the egg and milk mixture.

6 With adult help, fry the bread triangles in the oil until they are golden brown. Remove the bread triangles from the pan, and drain them on paper towels.

 7 Sprinkle the triangles with the cinnamon and sugar mixture. Enjoy!

11

CANADA

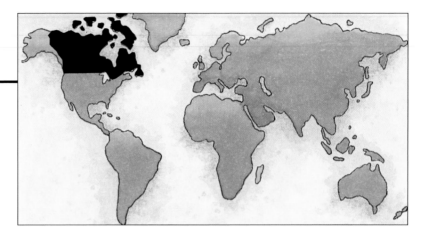

DATE: December 31 & January 1

NAME: New Year's

GREETING: Happy New Year, unless you live in Quebec, where the greeting is *Bonne Année*. This French greeting is pronounced bun ah-NAY .

On New Year's Eve some French Canadians go from house to house collecting food and clothes for needy people.

Then they return home with family and friends for a feast of roast turkey with chestnut pudding dressing and a raisin and nut pie. Many families gather to dance and sing to French-Canadian folk music played on fiddles or violins. Children often accompany the music by playing on spoons. They hit spoons to the music, while the adults perform a dance similar to the traditional American square dance.

Directions for making music with **SPOONS:**

WHAT YOU'LL NEED:

Spoons—wooden ones are the most authentic, but metal ones can be used, too

CD or cassette featuring folk music—if you can't find one that features French-Canadian folk music, Cajun music will sound similar to it

WHAT TO DO:

1 Listen to the music.

2 Hit your spoons to the rhythm and beat. Have some of your friends or family pair up and swing each other round and round.

In some families, children play a game with an orange that they pass around by their neck and chin. When the music stops, they stop passing it. Then the children begin to pass it when the music starts again. The children who can stay in the game the longest without dropping the orange are the winners. Try doing this to folk or square dance music.

13

CHILE

DATE: December 31 & January 1

NAME: Año Nuevo

GREETING: *Feliz Año Nuevo (Happy New Year)*
Pronounced fay-LEES AHN-yo new-EH-voh

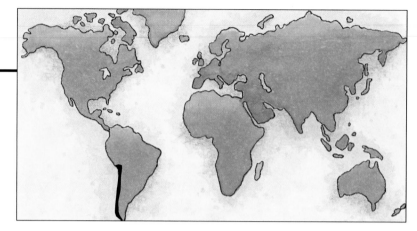

On New Year's Eve in Chile, your guests might arrive with a suitcase, but they don't plan to spend the night. The suitcase symbolizes good luck for the upcoming year. Some people even walk around the block with their suitcase twelve times to guarantee good luck for each month.

In addition to carrying suitcases, many people wear gold jewelry for good luck and make sure to have money in their pockets. They believe that this attracts prosperity for the year to come.

Make yourself a gold bracelet. Wear it on New Year's Eve and New Year's Day. It may bring you luck!

Directions for making a **GOLD BRACELET:**

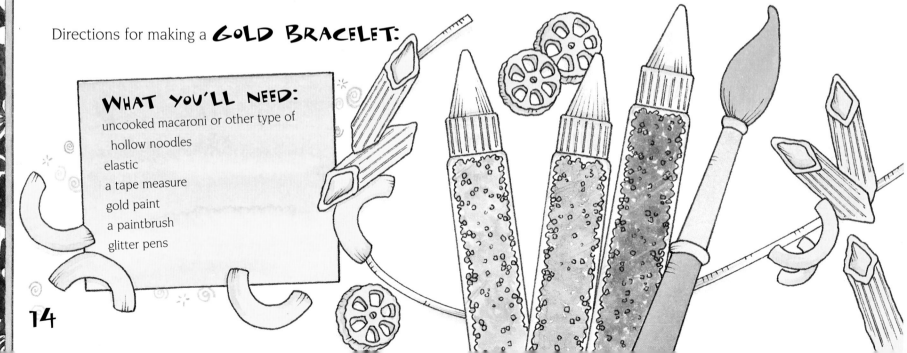

WHAT YOU'LL NEED:
uncooked macaroni or other type of
   hollow noodles
elastic
a tape measure
gold paint
a paintbrush
glitter pens

WHAT TO DO:

 1 Paint the noodles gold. Wait until they dry.

 2 Decorate the noodles with glitter pens.

 3 Measure your wrist, and add 1 inch (2.5 cm). You'll need this extra inch to tie the elastic. Then cut a piece of elastic that length.

4 String the decorated pasta onto the elastic.

5 Tie the elastic, and put your bracelet on.

In many Spanish-speaking countries, people eat twelve grapes at the stroke of midnight for good luck for each of the twelve months of the year. Here's how to say the name of the months in Spanish.

January — enero (eh-NEHR-oh)
February — febrero (feb-REHR-oh)
March — marzo (MAR-tsoh)
April — abril (ah-BREEL)
May — mayo (MAH-yoh)
June — junio (HOO-nee-oh)
July — julio (HOO-lee-oh)
August — agosto (aw-GOH-sto)
September — septiembre (sep-tee-EHM-bray)
October — octubre (ahk-TOO-bray)
November — noviembre (noh-vee-EHM-bray)
December — diciembre (dee-see-EHM-bray)

(In Spanish, the months don't begin with a capital letter as they do in English.)

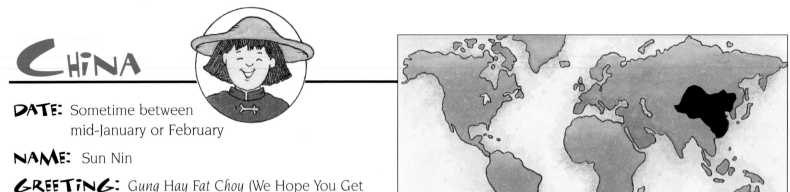

CHINA

DATE: Sometime between
mid-January or February

NAME: Sun Nin

GREETING: *Gung Hay Fat Choy* (We Hope You Get
Rich) Pronounced gung hay fat choy. The greeting is in
Cantonese, one of the major dialects of China. This
festival is celebrated by Chinese people living in many
parts of the world.

During the Chinese New Year, everyone turns a year older—even if their birthday happened the day
before the New Year began! The New Year is the most widely celebrated holiday in China. People call it
the Spring Festival. It lasts for fifteen days.

Chinese families clean their houses thoroughly before the Spring Festival and paste pictures of
the Kitchen God on the wall. They rub his lips with honey. They want him to report sweet things about
the family to the gods in heaven. During the weeks of the Spring Festival, people visit family and
friends. They wish them health, good luck, and happiness.

On the last day of New Year, people attend a parade led by a 100-foot (305-meter) dragon made
from bamboo and silk. About fifty men stand underneath the dragon to hold it. The dragon symbolizes
good luck and strength. Make some dragon puppets with your friends. Then parade around your home
or classroom saying, "Gung Hay Fat Choy!"

Directions for making a
DRAGON PUPPET:

WHAT YOU'LL NEED:
one sheet of red construction paper
one sheet of white construction paper
a wiggly eye (available at a craft store—or you can
    draw the eye on your dragon puppet)

glue
scissors
a craft stick
tape
a gold marking pen

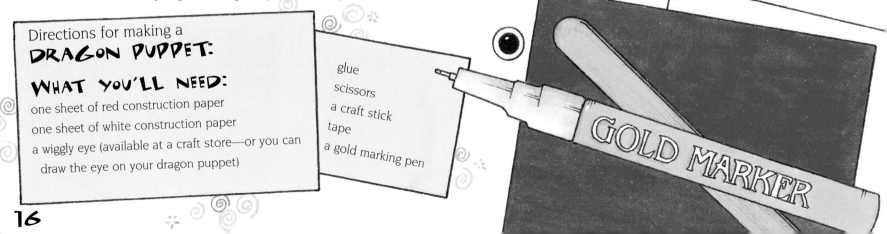

WHAT TO DO:

1 Fold the red paper in half lengthwise. Cut in half.

2 Fold one half of the paper accordion style. This will be the dragon's body.

3 Cut the dragon's head, tail, and fiery breath from the other half of the red sheet.

4 Cut horns from the white paper.

5 Glue the pieces together.

6 Glue on the wiggly eye.

7 Draw scales on the dragon with the gold pen.

8 Tape the craft stick to the dragon's body.

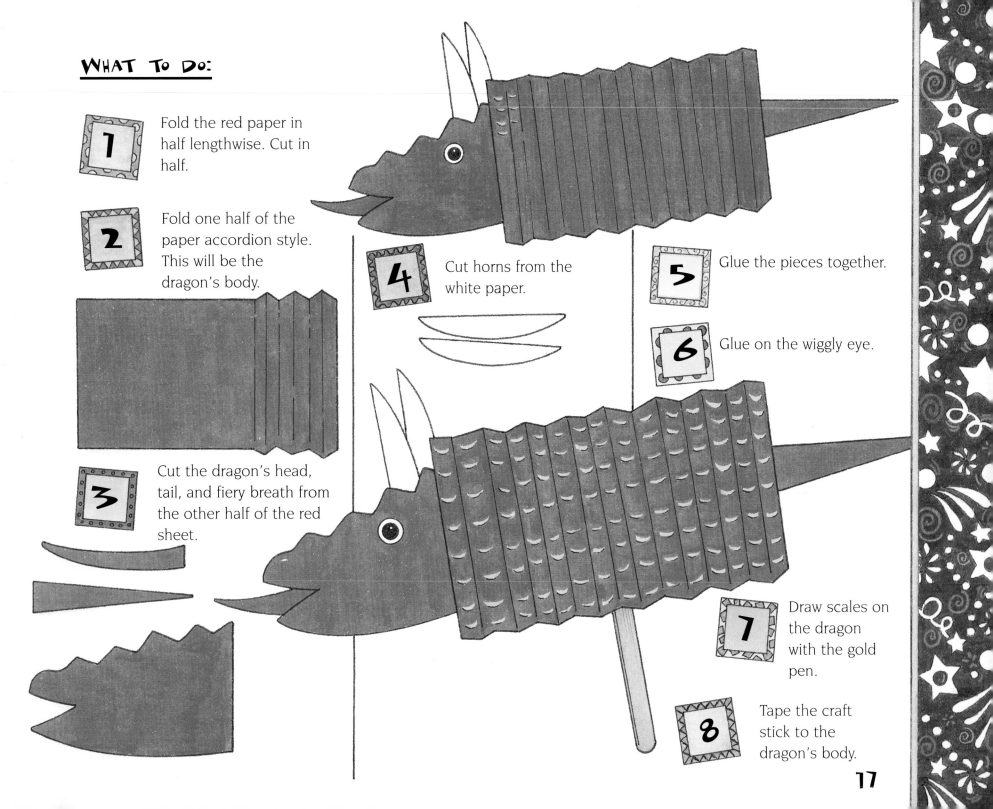

17

COLOMBIA

DATE: December 31 & January 1.

NAME: Año Nuevo

GREETING: *Feliz Año Nuevo* (Happy New Year)
Pronounced fay-LEES ahn-YO new-EH-voh

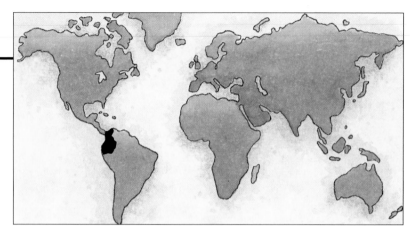

Colombian people wear yellow underwear on New Year's Eve and New Year's Day. They believe it brings health and good fortune in the upcoming year. Right before New Year's, you'll see lots of yellow underwear displayed in stores so people will buy it for the holiday.

Colombian people make wishes on New Year's Eve. They write them on slips of paper and put them inside elaborately decorated papier-mâché balloons called *globos* (glow-boes). They light a candle beneath the balloon. Then they watch the globos fly into the air and hope that their wishes come true.

You can make something similar to a globo.

Directions for making a **GLOBO:**

WHAT YOU'LL NEED:

a balloon
glue
white paper cut into strips about 1 inch
  (2.5 cm) wide
masking tape
string
stickers
tissue paper
ribbon
a slip of paper
wallpaper paste

WHAT TO DO:

 1 Blow up your balloon, and tie it tight.

 2 Tape your balloon to the end of a table. This way it won't wiggle as you attach the paper strips.

 3 Dip the strips of paper into the wallpaper paste. Attach them to the balloon. Make about 3 layers of strips.

 4 Hang the balloon to dry. This should take about 3 days.

Once your balloon is dry, you can decorate it. Here's how:

1 Decorate the tissue paper with drawings and/or stickers.

 2 Dab glue onto the balloon.

3 Glue the tissue paper onto your balloon.

4 Tie the end of the tissue paper to the balloon with the ribbon.

5 Write your wish on a slip of paper.

6 Tape your wish to the ribbon.

7 Keep your globo to remind yourself of your wish.

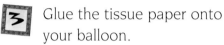

I wish I could have a cat!

ETHIOPIA

DATE: September 11 or 12, for two or three days

NAME: Enqutatash

GREETING: *Mel com Enqutatash* (Wishing you a Happy New Year) Pronounced mel calm en-koo-TAH-tash

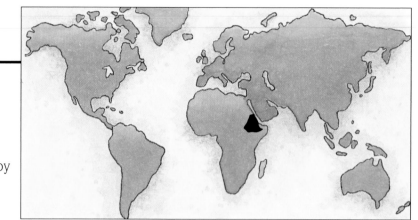

Ethiopians celebrate the new year at the end of their rainy season, when fields are full of flowers. *Enqutatash* means "gift of jewels." The evening before Enqutatash, people light torches made from branches and carry them to church. Then they jump over them. In the morning, many people wash away the old year by immersing their bodies in the nearest lake, river, or stream.

During Enqutatash, children visit their neighbors with armfuls of flowers. They receive money and sweets in return. If the person they are visiting is very special, they give him or her a rose, a symbol of Ethiopian patriotism.

Make a rose out of tissue paper. Give it to somebody special in your life.

Directions for making **ROSES:**

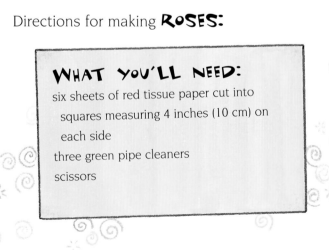

WHAT YOU'LL NEED:

six sheets of red tissue paper cut into
    squares measuring 4 inches (10 cm) on
    each side
three green pipe cleaners
scissors

The Ethiopian calendar has thirteen months. The first twelve months have 30 days each. The last month has five days unless it's a leap year. Then it has six.

WHAT TO DO:

 1 Layer the sheets of tissue paper on top of one another.

 2 Fold the papers like a fan.

 3 Tie the papers together with the first pipe cleaner.

 4 Pull the paper layers apart. Now you'll have a paper rose.

 5 Tie the bottom of your rose with the second pipe cleaner, and snip the edges of the pipe cleaner with your scissors.

6 Attach the third pipe cleaner to make a stem.

Make a few roses, and give somebody a bouquet.

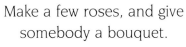

GERMANY

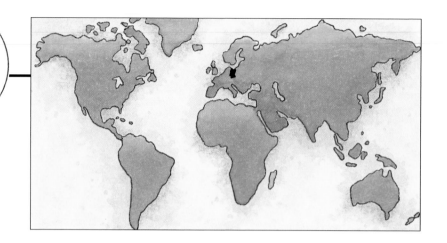

DATE: December 31 & January 1

NAME: Saint Sylvester Day or New Year's

GREETING: *Frohes Neues Jahr* (Happy New Year)
Pronounced FROY-es NOY-ess Yar

In Germany, on New Year's Eve, you might find miniature pigs, devils, chimney sweeps, or mushrooms in your home. They are made from plastic, wood, or an almond candy called marzipan. German people believe these figures are New Year's lucky charms. Some hosts and hostesses hire a chimney sweep or have a live pig attend their New Year's parties!

On New Year's Day or New Year's Eve many Germans like to predict what will happen to them during the upcoming year. Right before New Year's, they buy a special kind of lead that melts easily and let it drip into a bowl of cold water to cool. They look at the shapes of the cooled lead and guess what will happen to them during the upcoming year.

You can play a version of this game, too, by using a bowl of water and a candle.

How to play a **GERMAN FORTUNE-TELLING GAME:**

WHAT YOU'LL NEED:

6- to 8-inch (15- to 20-cm) candle—a dark
   color will work best
a small glass bowl of cold water

22

WHAT TO DO:

1 With adult help, light the candle.

2 Hold it over the water so the wax can fall into the water as it melts.

3 Watch the shapes that the wax makes as it cools.

Here's what some of the shapes might forecast:

An animal—maybe you'll get a new pet this year

An airplane or boat—maybe you'll go on a trip

A ring—maybe you'll be invited to a wedding

A ball—maybe your team will win an important game

A fish—maybe you'll learn to swim this year or get a swimming award at camp

Remember that fortune-telling doesn't really predict the future. It's just for fun.

GHANA

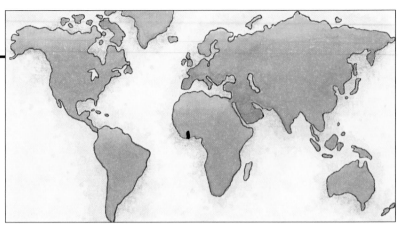

DATE: It begins the second or third Thursday in August and lasts through Sunday. It is celebrated by the Ga people of southern Ghana.

NAME: Homowo

GREETING: *Afee Aba Nina Woe* (Next year should come and meet us) Pronounced AH-fee AH-buh NIN-uh woh. English is the official language of Ghana, although many people speak a tribal language.

Homowo means "hooting at hunger," or it can mean "starved gods." During Homowo, people feast on steamed corn, palm nut soup, and fish. They sprinkle some of it on the ground to honor the gods and the spirits of their ancestors. Then they donate food to the less fortunate. Homowo is the new year of the harvest.

Ga people have family reunions during Homowo. They hold parades that feature triplets and twins, who wear whitish clay on their faces, and eat a meal of yams and eggs. Ga people consider twins and triplets a rare gift from the gods.

Homowo is a time of traditional dancing. Ga people dance to the sound of drums, bells, bamboo sticks, and shakers made from dried gourds. It takes almost a year for a gourd to dry out enough for the seeds to shake and make sounds.

You can make a shaker out of a balloon.

Directions for making a **BALLOON SHAKER:**

WHAT YOU'LL NEED:

a balloon

white paper cut into strips of about 1 inch (2.5 cm) wide

wallpaper paste

dried beans or rice

string

poster paint

a wide brush

a fine-tipped brush

masking tape

a pin

WHAT TO DO:

 1 Blow up the balloon to the size of a gourd.

 2 Tape the end of the balloon to a table. This way it won't wiggle as you work.

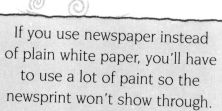 **3** Dip the strips of paper into the glue. Attach them to the balloon. Make about 3 layers of strips. Don't cover the end of the balloon.

 4 Hang the balloon to dry. This should take a day or two.

 5 When the balloon is dry, stick a pin in it to pop the balloon. Pour the beans or rice into the hole at the end of the balloon. Cover the hole with tape.

 **6** Paint your shaker.

If you use newspaper instead of plain white paper, you'll have to use a lot of paint so the newsprint won't show through.

You may want to rattle your shaker to a CD or cassette featuring African music.

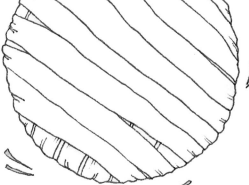

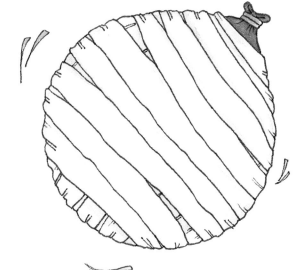

GREECE

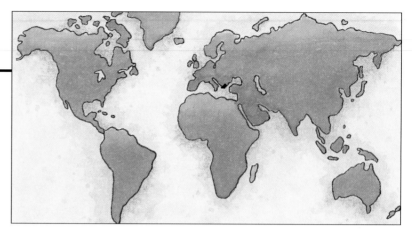

DATE: December 31 & January 1

NAME: The Feast of Saint Basil

GREETING: *Chronia Pollá* (Years many) Pronounced KRON-yah pole-AH

On New Year's Eve, Greek children line up their shoes in front of the fireplace. They hope that Saint Basil will come down the chimney to fill them with candy and toys. Greek people actually observe two holidays at once on December 31 and January 1: New Year's and the Feast of Saint Basil. Saint Basil is the patron saint of children. He died hundreds of years ago on January 1.

People attend parties. They give gifts and good luck charms to one another. Children go from house to house carrying tiny ships that represent the one Saint Basil sailed on. They sing a song called the Kalanda. At midnight, or sometimes on Saint Basil's Day, families eat a special bread called *vasilopita*. It has a coin hidden inside. The person who receives the slice containing it will have good luck for the upcoming year.

You can make a bread similar to vasilopita and serve it on New Year's Eve or New Year's Day.

Directions for making **VASILOPITA:**

WHAT YOU'LL NEED:
a package of refrigerated cinnamon
   roll dough
a cookie sheet or a loaf pan
slivered almonds

26

WHAT TO DO:

 With adult help, follow the directions on the package to make a loaf or sheet cake from the cinnamon roll dough.

 Wash a coin in soap and water. Wrap it in a piece of foil and hide it in the dough.

 When the loaf is done, frost it and decorate it with almonds. Some people arrange the almonds so that they'll spell out the number of the new year.

HAITI

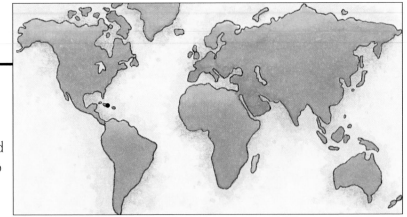

DATE: December 31 & January 1

NAME: Joudlan

GREETING: *Bòn Aneé* (Happy New Year) Pronounced bun ah-NAY. The greeting is in Creole, one of Haiti's two official languages. The other is French.

Haitian people often stay up on New Year's Eve to watch the sun rise. They are eagerly awaiting Joudlan. This is when Haitian people welcome the new year and celebrate their independence from France in 1804. New Year's in Haiti is similar to the Fourth of July in the United States. Families gather for special dinners, where they use their best dinnerware and tablecloths. Everyone in the family wears new clothes. Children receive gifts from their godparents.

On New Year's Day, many people gather in town squares. They listen to speakers discuss Haiti's history. They sing and dance to Haitian music. Everyone waves a Haitian flag to celebrate the new year and their country's independence.

You can make Haitian flags and wave them to celebrate Haiti's new year and independence.

Directions for making **HAITIAN FLAGS:**

WHAT YOU'LL NEED:

a sheet of red construction paper

a sheet of dark blue construction paper

glue

two craft sticks for each flag (6 sticks in all)

tape

WHAT TO DO:

 1 Fold each sheet of paper into thirds.

 2 Cut each sheet into three pieces.

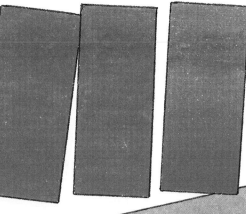

 3 Glue a blue sheet to a red sheet.

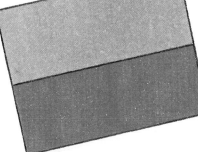 **4** Tape the craft sticks to the back of the flag. Make sure that you put tape going both up and down and across. Otherwise your flag stick will not be secure.

The colors in the flag stand for the people who fought for Haiti's independence. The blue symbolizes the Africans who had been brought over as slaves. The red symbolizes mixed-race Haitians.

If you want your flag to be really authentic, add a white square with a picture of a palm tree drawn on it to the center of the flag.

The materials will make three flags. Make one for yourself and two friends. Now you'll have Haitian flags similar to the kind Haitians wave on New Year's Day.

29

INDIA

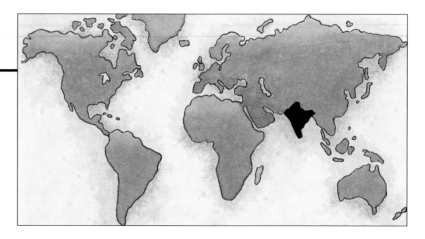

DATE: Sometime in October or November

NAME: Diwali

GREETING: *Sal Mubarak* (Wishing you a good new year) Pronounced sal muh-BAH-rahk. The greeting is in Gujarati, one of India's languages. The Hindu religion is one of the major religions of India. Diwali is a Hindu holiday often celebrated by Hindu people living in countries other than India.

During Diwali, there are rows of tiny oil lamps, called *divas*, inside and outside every home. *Diwali* means "cluster of lights." Indian people believe the lamps invite Lakshmi, the goddess of wealth and prosperity, to bless their homes. Many families light at least fifty divas to make sure that Lakshmi arrives.

Before Diwali, Indian people pay off their debts. They give gifts and send cards. The cards usually have pictures of divas or Lakshmi on them and contain wishes for good fortune.

Make a diva and hope that Lakshmi brings you good luck.

Directions for making a **DIVA:**

WHAT YOU'LL NEED:
clay—the kind that hardens and is not flammable
poster paint
a paintbrush
sequins
glue glitter pens, optional
a votive candle

WHAT TO DO:

 Shape the clay into a ball, about the size of a golf ball.

 Poke your fingers into the center to make the ball into a bowl-shaped container. Press in the sequins well.

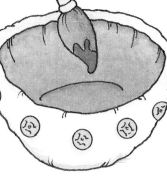

 When your diva dries, paint it.

 When the paint dries, dab on blobs of glitter glue. Spread the glitter blobs over the diva with your fingers.

When the glitter dries, place the candle inside the diva. With adult help, light it.

IRAN

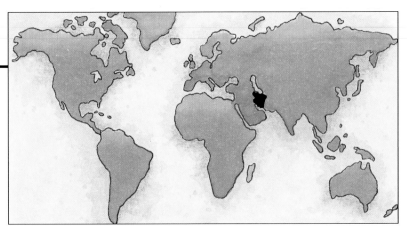

DATE: Begins April 20 or 21 and lasts for thirteen days

NAME: Nouruz

GREETING: *Aideh Shoma Mobarac* (Happy Celebration) Pronounced eye-DEH show-MAH mah-bar-ACK. The greeting is in Persian, one of the languages spoken in Iran.

Iranian children welcome New Year's on the first day of spring. They call it *Nouruz*, which means "new day."

Two weeks before Nouruz, Iranian families plant a *sabzeh*, a pot of wheat or lentil seeds. By the time Nouruz arrives, the seeds sprout and symbolize new life and good fortune. On the last day of Nouruz everyone leaves home for a picnic. During the picnic, people dump their sabzeh into a nearby river, stream, lake, or running water. They believe this gets rid of any bad luck from the past year—and it ensures good luck for the new one.

Directions for making a **SABZEH:**

WHAT YOU'LL NEED:

a paper cup

potting soil

wheat, lentil, or grass seeds

WHAT TO DO:

1 Fill your cup with potting soil.

2 Sprinkle a lot of seeds on top. Sprinkle more soil over the seeds, just enough to cover them.

3 Moisten your sabzeh with water.

4 Put it in a sunny place.

5 Water it daily.

The seeds in your sabzeh will begin to grow in a few days.

During Nouruz, families set up a table with seven objects that begin with the letter "S." It usually includes:

- *Samanoo* (sweet wheat pudding)
- *Sumac* (dried crushed berries)
- *Sekkeh* (gold coin) or *seam* (silver coin)
- *Seeb* (apple)
- *Serkeh* (vinegar)
- *Somul* (a flower)
- *Senjeb* (olives)

A bowl of goldfish, colored hard-boiled eggs, and a mirror are also on the table.

Israel

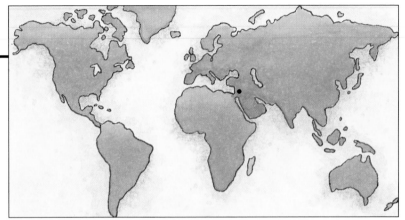

DATE: Sometime in September or October

NAME: Rosh Hashanah

GREETING: *L'shanah Tovah* (Good Year) Pronounced luh-shah-NAH toe-VAH. Rosh Hashanah is not only observed in Israel; it's celebrated by Jewish people all over the world. Hebrew is Israel's main language.

Some people refer to Rosh Hashanah as the world's birthday. It means "head of the year." Rosh Hashanah begins ten days of repentance. During this time Jewish people ask forgiveness from other people for any wrongs they might have done them during the past year.

The last day of repentance is Yom Kippur, the Day of Atonement. It's the holiest day of the year. Adults spend the day in synagogue, the Jewish place of worship. They spend the day in prayer, and do not eat or drink anything until sundown.

On the eve of Rosh Hashanah, the family sits down to a special dinner. It includes sweet foods such as honey cookies, kugel (a baked dish often made with noodles and raisins), and apples dipped in honey. By eating these foods, people hope that the new year will be sweet and filled with happiness.

Dip apples into honey and wish a sweet year for yourself.

Directions for making **APPLES DIPPED IN HONEY:**

WHAT YOU'LL NEED:

an apple
a jar of honey
a dish
a knife
an apple corer
two plates

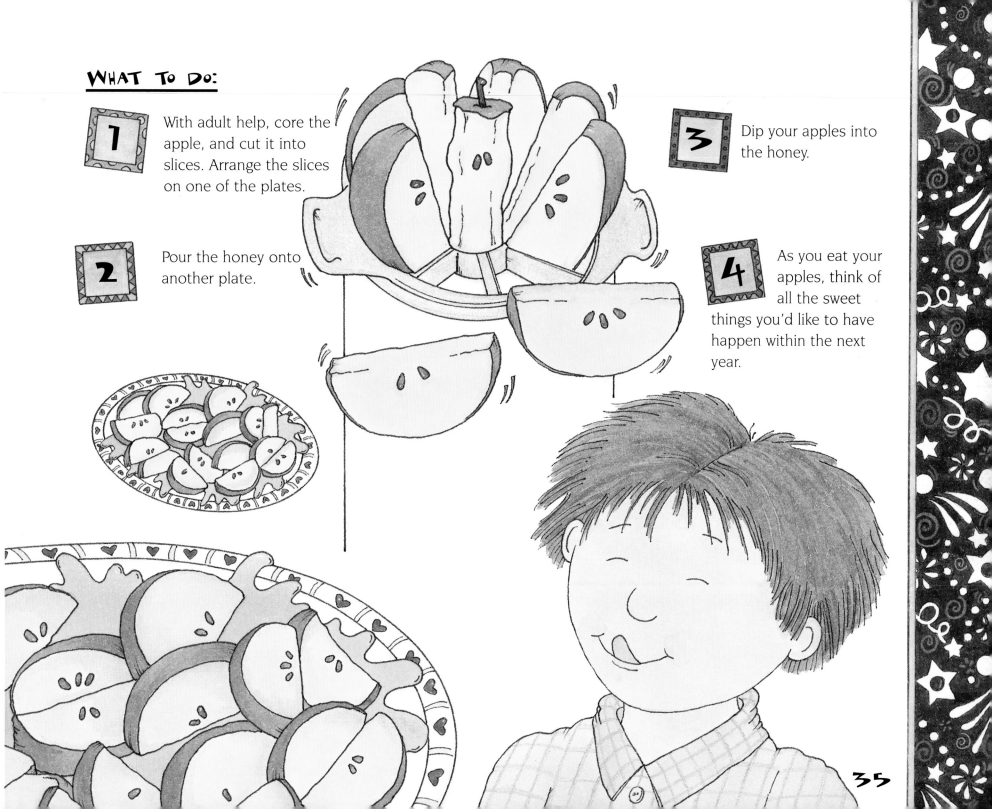

WHAT TO DO:

1 With adult help, core the apple, and cut it into slices. Arrange the slices on one of the plates.

2 Pour the honey onto another plate.

3 Dip your apples into the honey.

4 As you eat your apples, think of all the sweet things you'd like to have happen within the next year.

35

JAPAN

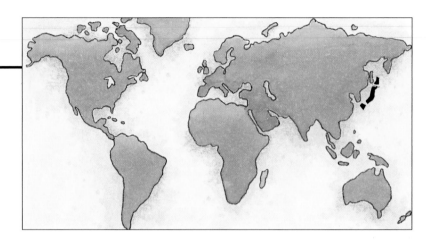

DATE: December 31, lasts for 3 to 7 days

NAME: Oshogatsu

GREETING: *Akemashite omedeto gozaimasu* (Congratulations, the new year has come) Pronounced ah-keh-mash-TEH oh-meh-deh-toe go-zay-ee-mah-suh

During Oshogatsu, many Japanese children and adults receive a doll with no eyes on it. They paint one eye on the doll and make a wish. They add the second one during the year when their wish comes true.

Oshogatsu is one of the biggest holidays in Japan. People decorate their homes with good luck symbols. They hang a rice straw rope at the entrance of their homes to protect against evil spirits entering. They eat long noodles and try to swallow them whole—to ensure a long life. Everyone sends New Year's cards, which the post office tries its best to deliver on January 1.

Children play special games during Oshogatsu such as *Fuku Wari*. It's similar to Pin the Tail on the Donkey. Here's how to play it.

How to play **FUKU WARI:**

Number of players: 2 to 6

WHAT YOU'LL NEED:

2 large sheets of paper

a marker

scissors

masking tape or pins

a blindfold

WHAT TO DO:

 1 Draw an outline of a head on one sheet of paper.

 2 Draw a picture of a pair of eyes, ears, a nose, and a mouth on the second sheet of paper. Then cut them out.

Now you are ready to play Fuku Wari.

At midnight on New Year's Eve, people wait for the sound of a gong. It rings 108 times to chase away 108 sins. People laugh, giggle, and smile while the gong rings. They hope that their happiness will bring them good luck for the new year.

1 Tape the picture of the face on the wall.

2 Give the players the ears, eyes, nose, and mouth.

3 Have each player attempt to attach the missing parts of the face to the blank face while blindfolded.

37

MEXICO

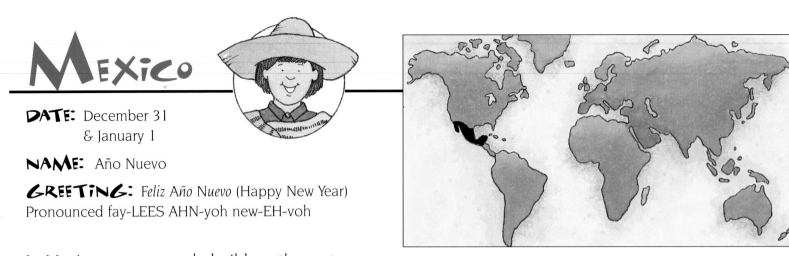

DATE: December 31
& January 1

NAME: Año Nuevo

GREETING: *Feliz Año Nuevo* (Happy New Year)
Pronounced fay-LEES AHN-yoh new-EH-voh

In Mexico, some people build castles or towers
from sticks of wood especially for the new year. They string them with firecrackers. At midnight on December 31, they light their creations to welcome the new year and listen to the fireworks explode. All over Mexico at the stroke of twelve on December 31, there are displays of fireworks and the sound of firecrackers, horns, and bells. In many homes, people quickly eat twelve grapes or raisins the moment midnight comes. They believe this brings good luck for each month of the new year.

At the stroke of twelve, eat twelve grapes as fast as you can. Count to twelve in Spanish, and say the names of the months in Spanish, too. Here's how to do it.

Months

January	enero
February	febrero
March	marzo
April	abril
May	mayo
June	junio
July	julio
August	agosto
September	septiembre
October	octubre
November	noviembre
December	diciembre

(See Chile for the pronunciation of the months in Spanish.)

Numbers

one	uno (OO-noh)
two	dos (DOSE)
three	tres (TRACE)
four	cuatro (KWAH-troh)
five	cinco (SING-koh)
six	seis (SACE)
seven	siete (see-EH-tay)
eight	ocho (OH-choh)
nine	nueve (noo-EH-vay)
ten	diez (dee-ACE)
eleven	once (OHN-say)
twelve	doce (DOE-say)

NiGERiA

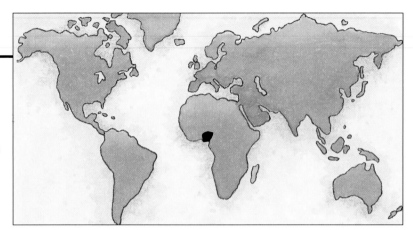

DATE: December 31 & January 1

NAME: New Year's

GREETiNG: *Tugberuh* (How are you doing?)
Pronounced tug-BEAR-uh. This greeting is in the language
of the Ijaw people. The major language of Nigeria is
English, but many people also use a tribal language.

The Ijaw people of Nigeria wait until midnight on
December 31 to scare away evil spirits from the old year. They want to make sure that no bad luck
follows them into the new year. People shake trees. They dust everything in their homes well. They
beat on walls and bang on pots and pans. They hope all the commotion makes the spirits go away.

Some people throw old dishes and clothes in the river to make sure that any bad luck they
contain washes away forever. People wear masks and costumes to scare away spirits, too. They make
sure that the masks are frightening enough to make the spirits leave for an entire year.

You can make a scary mask. Wear it on New Year's or any time of the year to frighten any evil
spirits—or your friends.

Directions for making a **MASK:**

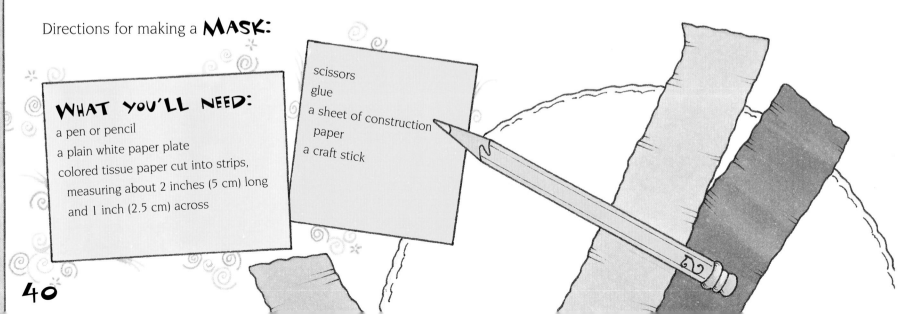

WHAT YOU'LL NEED:

a pen or pencil
a plain white paper plate
colored tissue paper cut into strips,
   measuring about 2 inches (5 cm) long
   and 1 inch (2.5 cm) across

scissors
glue
a sheet of construction
   paper
a craft stick

WHAT TO DO:

 1 Cut out the construction paper so that it covers the center of the paper plate. Glue onto the plate.

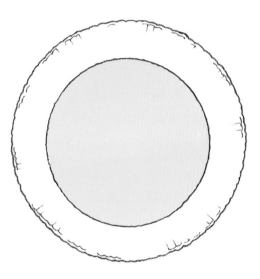

 2 While it's drying, you can cut out the strips of construction paper.

 3 When the construction paper is dry, draw the spaces where you'd like the mouth and nose to go. Then cut them out.

 4 Glue the tissue paper strips to the paper plate.

 5 Glue the craft stick to the back of the mask.

Scotland

DATE: December 31 and January 1

NAME: Hogmanay

GREETING: Happy New Year!
Scotland's language is English.

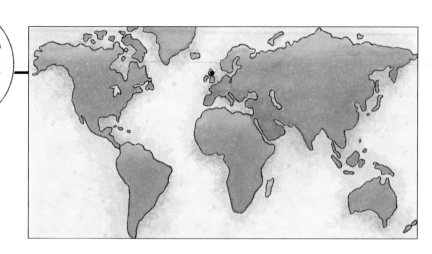

You've probably heard the song "Auld Lang Syne." It originated in Scotland. It's based on a poem written by Robert Burns, Scotland's national poet.

In Scotland's largest cities, Edinburgh and Glasgow, people buy tickets to huge New Year's Eve street parties. More than 200,000 people attend. They light New Year's bonfires and follow parades led by people carrying torches. At midnight, everyone kisses. Then, they hold hands, stand in a circle, sing "Auld Lang Syne," and kiss again. But, they wait until the stroke of midnight to kiss or sing. It's considered bad luck to say Happy New Year or sing aloud before the old year is gone.

Here are the words to "Auld Lang Syne." Stand in a circle, and sing it.

The word *auld* means "old." *Lang* means "long." *Syne* means "since," or "long ago."

Should auld ac-quain-tance be for-got And nev - er brought to mind? Should

auld ac-quain-tance be for - got And days of auld lang syne!

Chorus:

For auld lang syne, my dear, For auld lang syne, We'll

take a cup o' kind - ness yet For auld lang syne.

TRINIDAD & TOBAGO

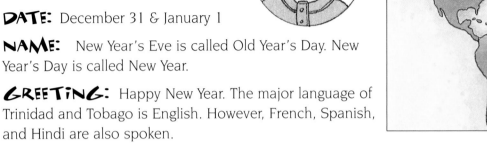

DATE: December 31 & January 1

NAME: New Year's Eve is called Old Year's Day. New Year's Day is called New Year.

GREETING: Happy New Year. The major language of Trinidad and Tobago is English. However, French, Spanish, and Hindi are also spoken.

On Old Year's Day, at midnight, people light bamboo sticks. The lit bamboo sticks make a loud sound similar to firecrackers. The sound is a way of saying good-bye to the old year and welcoming the new one. Old Year's festivities often begin as early as three or four in the afternoon with steel drum bands traveling from house to house, playing traditional Caribbean music. Steel drums are made from sawed-off oil drums that are pounded, grooved, and tuned. Some people invite the drummers into their homes and give them a drink called sorrel, which is similar to sweetened cranberry juice.

You can make instruments similar to steel drums with an empty cookie, popcorn, or candy tin. A tall can will make a low sound. A short one will make a high one.

Directions for making **STEEL DRUMS:**

WHAT YOU'LL NEED:

empty food tins, the kind that once contained
  popcorn, candy, or cookies
poster paint—steel drums are often painted
  metallic silver, but they come in other colors
a paintbrush
a 6-inch (15-cm) dowel stick
rubber bands

WHAT TO DO:

1 Paint your tin.

2 Tie rubber bands to the end of the dowel sticks so that they cover the ends.

3 When the paint dries, hit your tin with the dowel stick.

If you can, beat your drums to a CD or cassette featuring Caribbean music.

caribbean Music

45

Vietnam

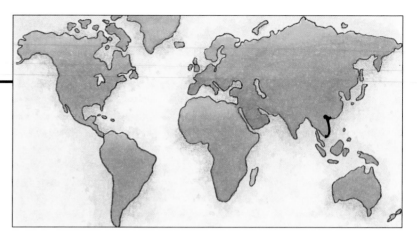

DATE: Sometime between January 19 and February 20. Lasts three days.

NAME: Tet

GREETING: *Chuc Mung Nam Moi* (Good wishes to you for the New Year) Pronounced chock moung num moo-EE

How would you like to receive money on New Year's? During Tet, Vietnamese children do. Their parents and grandparents give them red envelopes filled with lucky money and wishes for good luck. The envelopes are called *li xi* (lee see). Even babies receive li xi.

Vietnamese people consider Tet everybody's birthday. So everyone turns a year older. During Tet, people give gifts of candy and flowers and fruit to relatives, teachers, bosses, and friends. They send cards to one another. They eat special foods like *mut*, a candy made from dried fruits or vegetables. They decorate their homes with long red sheets of paper that have New Year's wishes written on them.

Make some New Year's wishes. Write them on long sheets of red paper. Hang your banners in your classroom or house.

Directions for making **BANNERS:**

WHAT YOU'LL NEED:

a black fine-tipped marker

a pen that writes in gold

sheets of red paper, measuring about 6 inches (15 cm) wide to about 15 inches (38 cm) long

WHAT TO DO:

 Practice writing your wishes so that they'll be in your best handwriting.

 Turn the paper vertically, and write your wishes on it.

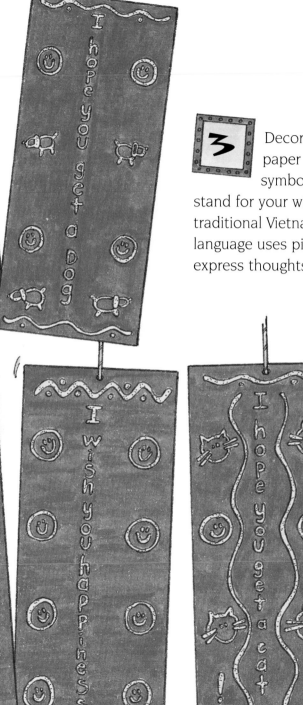

3 Decorate the paper with symbols that stand for your wish. The traditional Vietnamese language uses pictures to express thoughts and ideas.

47

BiBLioGRAPHY

———: *Festivals in Asia*, Kodansha International, Ltd., Tokyo, New York, San Francisco, 1975.

———: *Israel* (*Fiesta!*), Grolier Educational, Danbury, CT, 1997.

———: *More Festivals in Asia*, Kodansha International, Ltd., Tokyo, New York, San Francisco, 1975.

Adeloye, Anthony, Consultant: *Nigeria* (*Fiesta!*), Grolier Educational, Danbury, CT, 1997.

Behrens, June: *Gung Hay Fat Choy*, Children's Press, Chicago, 1982.

Bernhard, Emery: *Happy New Year!*, Lodestar Books, New York, 1996.

Blackwood, Alan: *New Year* (*Holidays & Festivals*), Rourke Enterprises, Inc., Vero Beach, FL, 1987.

Campbell, Louisa: *A World of Holidays*, Silver Moon Press, New York, 1993.

Dalal, Anita, Consultant, and Berta Villamandos: *Guatemala* (*Fiesta!*), Grolier Educational, Danbury, CT, 1999.

Debebe, Negash, and Habte Lakew, Consultant, The Ethiopian Orthodox Church, London: *Ethiopia* (*Fiesta!*), Grolier Educational, Danbury, CT, 1999.

Demi: *Happy New Year! Kung-Hsi Fa-Ts'ai!*, Crown Publishers, New York, 1997.

Fabres, Ana, Consultant: *Brazil* (*Fiesta!*), Grolier Educational, Danbury, CT, 1997.

Groh, Lynn: *New Year's Day* (*A Holiday Book*), Garrard Publishing Company, Champaign, IL, 1964.

Henderson, Helene, and Sue Ellen Thompson, Editors: *Holidays, Festivals, and Celebrations of the World Dictionary*, Second Edition, Omnigraphics, Inc., Detroit, MI, 1997.

Johnson, Lois S.: *Happy New Year Around the World*, Rand McNally, Chicago, New York, San Francisco, 1966.

Kalman, Bobbie: *We Celebrate New Year*, Crabtree Pub. Co., Toronto, New York, 1985.

Kanitkar, V. P.: *India* (*Fiesta!*), Grolier Educational, Danbury, CT, 1999.

Kelley, Emily: *Happy New Year*, Carolrhoda Books, Minneapolis, MN, 1984.

Kindersley, Barnabas and Anabel: *Children Just Like Me Celebrations!*, DK Publishing Inc., New York, 1997.

Luenn, Nancy: *Celebrations of Light*, Atheneum Books for Young Readers, An Imprint of Simon & Schuster Children's Publishing Division, New York, 1998.

Moyse, Sarah: *Chinese New Year*, The Millbrook Press, Brookfield, CT, 1996.

Myers, Robert J., and The Editors of Hallmark Cards: *Celebrations: The Complete Book of American Holidays*, Doubleday & Company, Garden City, NY, 1972.

Nguyen, Tuyen, Consultant: *Vietnam* (*Fiesta!*), Grolier Educational, Danbury, CT, 1997.

Potter, Heidi, and Rachel Tiffin, Consultant: *Japan* (*Fiesta!*), Grolier Educational, Danbury, CT, 1997.

Roraff, Susan: *Festivals of the World: Chile*, Gareth Stevens Publishing, Milwaukee, WI, 1998.

Rosen, Mike: *Spring Festivals* (*Seasonal Festivals*), The Bookwright Press, New York, 1991.

Sayer, Chloë, Consultant: *Mexico* (*Fiesta!*), Grolier Educational, Danbury, CT, 1997.

Sidras, Efstathia: *Festivals of the World: Greece*, Gareth Stevens Publishing, Milwaukee, WI, 1998.

Silverthorne, Elizabeth: *Fiesta! Mexico's Great Celebrations*, The Millbrook Press, Brookfield, CT, 1992.

Thompson, Paul, Consultant, and Sayron Lao: *Cambodia* (*Fiesta!*), Grolier Educational, Danbury, CT, 1999.

Viesti, Joe, and Diana Hall: *Celebrate! In Southeast Asia*, Lothrop, Lee & Shepard Books, New York, 1996.

Wangyal, Riga, Consultant, Tibet Foundation, London: *Tibet* (*Fiesta!*), Grolier Educational, Danbury, CT, 1999.

Winchester, Faith: *Asian Holidays*, Bridgestone Books, Imprint of Capstone Press, Mankato, MN, 1996.

Ziegler, Sandra, Editor: *Special Holidays Handbook*, The Child's World, Elgin, IL, 1986.